Grammar Copymasters

Contents

How to use this book 3

1 - Sentence punctuation
1.1 Capital letters and full stops 4
1.2 Question mark 6
1.3 Exclamation marks 9
1.4 Commas for lists 13
1.5a Apostrophes - possessive 14
1.5b Apostrophes - contractions 17

2 - Writing sentences
2.1 Joining words and clauses using the conjunction **and** 20
2.2 Coordinating and subordinating conjunctions 23
2.3 Nouns, Simple noun phrases, Expanded noun phrases 26
2.4 Statements, questions, exclamations, commands 30

3 - Prefixes and suffixes
3.1 Plural noun suffixes: **-s**, **-es** 33
3.2 Verbs, Suffixes added to verbs 35
3.3 Prefix **un-** 39
3.4 Suffixes to form nouns: **-er**, **-ness** 41
3.5 Compound nouns 44
3.6 Suffixes to form adjectives: **-ful**, **-less** 47
3.7 Suffixes to form adjectives: **-er**, **-est** 49
3.8 Suffixes to form adverbs: **-ly** 53

4 - Tenses
4.1 Present and past tenses 57
4.2 Present progressive and past tenses 61

Published by Letterland International Ltd, Leatherhead, Surrey, KT22 9AD, UK.
www.letterland.com

ISBN 978-1-78248-165-2
Product Code: TH86

© Letterland International Ltd 2016
LETTERLAND® is a registered trademark of Lyn Wendon.

10 9 8 7 6 5 4 3 2 1

Written by Lucy Marcovitch & Lisa Holt
Designed by Laura Bittles
Originator of Letterland: Lyn Wendon

Sassoon Infant is a typeface designed for children learning to read and write.
© Adrian Williams Design Ltd

Any educational institution that has purchased one copy of this publication may make duplicate copies for use exclusively within that institution. Permission does not extend to reproduction, storage in a retrieval system, or transmittal, in any form or by any means, electronic, mechanical, photocopying, recording or otherwise, of duplicate copies for loaning, renting or selling to any other institution without either the prior consent in writing of the Publisher or a licence permitting restricted copying in the United Kingdom issued by the Copyright Licensing Agency Ltd, 90 Tottenham Court Road, London W1T 4LP. This book is sold subject to the condition that it shall not by way of trade or otherwise be lent, hired out or otherwise circulated without the Publisher's prior consent.

British Library Cataloguing in Publication Data
A Catalogue record for this publication is available from the British Library.

Printed in the UK

How to use this book

These *Grammar Copymasters* are designed to consolidate and extend the teaching content of the *Letterland Grammar Teacher's Guide*. All Units of the guide, including sentence punctuation, writing sentences, prefixes and suffixes, and tenses are covered. The *Copymasters* provide an excellent resource for individual or group work. They are also useful as an activity for children working with parents or helpers.

The *Copymasters* provide activities for various levels of attainment. They can also be used as a stepping-stone towards more open-ended tasks. For example, once children have completed the activities on a sheet, you may like to ask them to make up their own sentences using some of the punctuation or grammatical techniques they have just learned about. Or see how many words of the same structure they can find in books, magazines or newspapers.

The *Letterland Grammar Teacher's Guide* is the recommended starting point for introducing each new grammatical concept. You could plan your teaching as follows:

- Decide on the grammar concept you are going to teach and work through the suggested activities in the *Grammar Teacher's Guide*.
- Look at the *Examples* for the lesson on the *Grammar Resources CD* or in the Appendices of the *Teacher's Guide*. Work through the first examples together as a class.
- Give out copies of the relevant copymaster to a group or the whole class.
- Go over the instructions on the copymaster. Encourage the children to re-read the instructions carefully and aim to master all the instruction vocabulary as soon as possible so they can work through the sheets independently.
- During another group session, go over the main teaching points to assess understanding.

1.1 Capital letters and full stops

Underline where the **capital letters** should be in these sentences.

1. that snowman has a top hat.

2. there are ten ducks on the pond.

3. my sister is good at magic tricks.

4. gran has a red front door.

5. we went to the park to ride our bikes.

Use **full stops** to show where these sentences end.

1. There are lots of flowers in that garden

2. I like playing on the swings

3. We saw a crab on the beach

4. My sister is older than me She is ten

5. This is a good book I have read it twice

Name: _____ Date: _____

1.1 *(continued)*
Capital letters and full stops

Add **full stops** and underline where the **capital letters** should be to make these sentences correct.

1. my new shoes make a funny sound

2. she ran quickly to the top of the hill

3. there is a nest in that bush

4. my sister likes reading books about castles

5. that is my red pencil

Match the pictures to the correct sentences. Write the number in the box.

1.2a
Question marks

Put a **question mark**, where necessary, in the correct place.

1. Why are you splashing me

2. Is the train coming soon

3. Did you see the frog in the pond

4. That cat is up in the tree

5. May I please have some cake

6. Are we going to the beach yet

7. It is going to be hot today

8. What is your name

9. Who won the race

10. Please will you pass me a pen

1.2a (continued)
Question marks and full stops

Correct these sentences using either **full stops** or **question marks**.

1. Did that cat jump out of the tree

2. The cat landed on its feet

3. I went swimming in the sea

4. Did you enjoy your trip

5. When are you going on holiday

6. It is nearly my birthday

7. Would you like to bake some biscuits

8. Why is she crying

9. I like your new robot toy

10. Can I borrow your umbrella please

Name: _____ Date: _____

1.2b
Question marks

Put a tick next to the **questions**.   (✓)

1. How old are you? ☐
2. Can you bounce the ball? ☐
3. She can bounce the ball ten times. ☐
4. Dippy Duck lives in a duck pond. ☐
5. Can you hear a duck quacking? ☐
6. My brother keeps bees in a hive. ☐
7. Does she like honey on her toast? ☐
8. Can we go to the park now? ☐
9. How many legs do you have? ☐
10. I enjoy sitting in the sun. ☐

Now write three **questions** of your own. Don't forget the **question mark**!

1. _____

2. _____

3. _____

1.3a
Exclamation marks

Put an **exclamation mark** in the correct place.

1. Stop splashing me
2. Here comes the train
3. Look at that frog
4. You silly cat – come down
5. I want some chocolate cake
6. It's so hot today
7. Look at Sammy go
8. Max can fix anything
9. That's impossible
10. The house is on fire

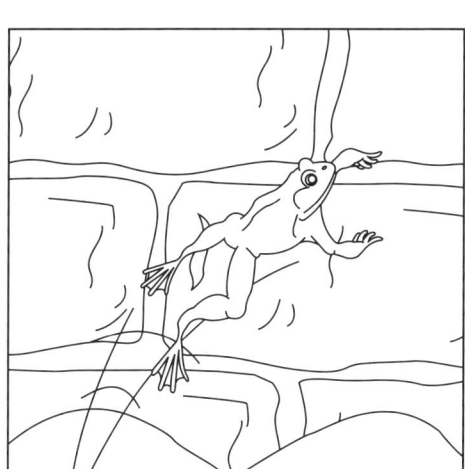

Name: _____ Date: _____

1.3a *(continued)*
Exclamation marks and full stops

Complete these sentences using either **exclamation marks** or **full stops**.

1. The cat jumped out of the tree

2. That was amazing

3. I went swimming in the sea

4. She went on holiday

5. I can't wait until my birthday

6. Thank you for my present

7. The magician was incredible

8. I like your new robot toy

9. That baby is so noisy

10. Don't do that

1.3a (continued)
Exclamation marks

Put a tick next to the **exclamations**. (✓)

1. Stop fighting!
2. I like eating pizza.
3. He is such a fast runner!
4. Jim can juggle and jump!
5. My hat blew off!
6. I'd like to go to the park after school.
7. Happy birthday!
8. My kite got stuck in the tree.
9. Help me!
10. Nick is so noisy!

Now write three **exclamations** of your own. Remember the **exclamation mark**!

1. _____

2. _____

3. _____

1.3b Exclamations and questions

Add an **exclamation** or **question mark** to make these sentences correct.

1. Where is he
2. Watch out
3. Did James bake that chocolate cake
4. Who won the swimming race
5. She is so fast
6. Could I have a drink please
7. Can you stand on one leg
8. I do not want you to go
9. Help him
10. Look at that cute puppy

Now can you write two **exclamations** and one **question** of your own? Don't forget the correct punctuation mark at the end!

1. _____
2. _____
3. _____

1.4 Commas for lists

Place the missing **commas** in these lists.

1. I like to eat apples grapes peaches and nuts.

2. There are pens pencils and a ruler in my bag.

3. The shop sells fruit vegetables meat and fish.

4. Mike the monster likes munching on melon mangoes marshmallows mushrooms and metal!

5. The girl is wearing a red skirt red shirt and red socks.

6. At my birthday party we are having crisps pizza carrots grapes and cake.

7. I collect sticks acorns pebbles and leaves.

8. I drew a picture using pens pencils and paints.

9. My best friends are Lucy Ella Abdul and Samina.

10. I saw Harry Sammy and Nick having a race.

Note: A Serial comma (also called Oxford or Harvard comma) is a comma placed immediately before the coordinating conjunction (usually **and**, **or**, or **nor**) in a series of three or more terms. Most commonly British English publications do not use the Serial comma.

Name: _____ Date: _____

1.5a
Apostrophes - possessive

Put the **apostrophes** in the right place to show who the object belongs to.

1. Kates fast car
2. Tims toys
3. The robots left arm
4. My cats milk
5. The queens palace
6. Dads book
7. My sisters room
8. Grandmas bag
9. Mums computer
10. My brothers shoes

Now try completing these sentences. Don't forget the **apostrophe**!

1. Lucy has lost her lamb. Where is _____ lamb?
2. Harry has lots of hats. They are all _____ hats.
3. Jim has a new jeep. It is _____ jeep.
4. Nick can play his drums. They are _____ drums.

Name: _____ Date: _____

1.5a *(continued)*

Apostrophes - possessive

Now try completing these sentences. Don't forget the **apostrophe**!

1. The teacher is reading her book.
   It is the _____ book.

2. The cat lives with Klara. She is _____ cat.

3. Mark has one girl. He is the _____ dad.

4. Max is reading a book with a red cover.
   The _____ cover is red.

5. The shop on the street has an open door.
   The _____ door is open.

6. I am flying my kite. The _____ tail is fluttering in the sky.

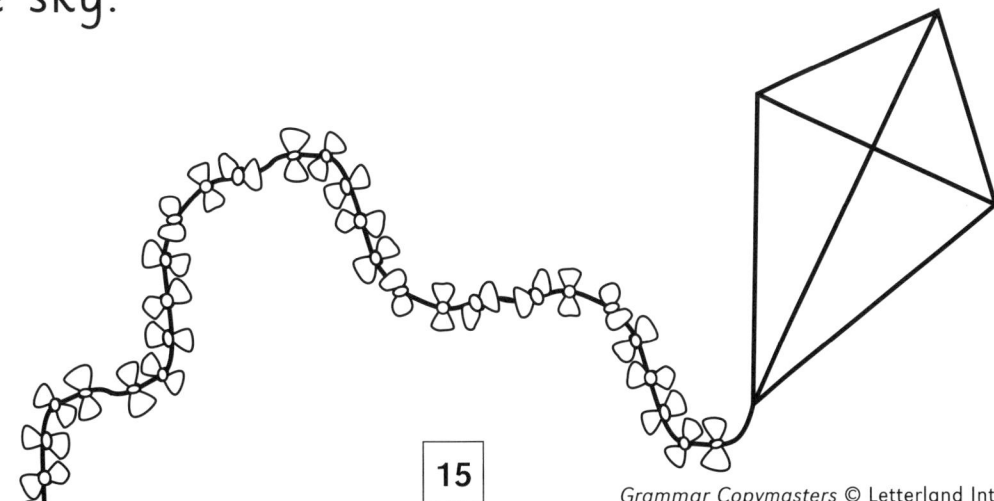

1.5a (continued)

Apostrophes - possessive

Cross out the incorrect word to complete the sentences.

1. ~~Lucys~~ Lucy's light is lovely.

2. Vicky's ~~Vickys~~ van is very shiny.

3. Fred's ~~Freds~~ fire engine can go very fast.

4. That ~~cars~~ car's tyre is flat.

5. The boy's ~~boys~~ bag is red.

6. The ~~girls~~ girl's eyes are brown.

7. The ~~childrens~~ children's playground has a zip wire.

8. Her ~~hamsters~~ hamster's wheel is squeaky.

9. The king's ~~kings~~ legs are longer than ~~Nicks~~ Nick's legs.

10. Dad's ~~Dads~~ beard is prickly.

Name: _____ Date: _____

1.5b
Apostrophes - contractions

Can you join the correct **contraction** to these words?

I am	We're
We are	I've
They are	He's
I have	I'd
She would	It's
It is	She'd
He is	I'm
I would	They're

Now do it the other way round! Join the words to the correct **contraction**.

Haven't	She will
Let's	We would
She'll	Is not
We'd	That is
We'll	Have not
Isn't	Do not
Don't	Let us
That's	We will

17

Grammar Copymasters © Letterland International Ltd.

1.5b (continued)

Apostrophes - contractions

Write the correct **contraction** for the bold words in these sentences.

1. **We will** go to the cinema later on.
2. You **must not** eat that cake!
3. **She is** such a cute bunny!
4. **I would** like to go swimming.
5. The cat **can not** get down!
6. **Do not** go near the hot water!
7. The duck **was not** sitting on her eggs when we walked past.
8. **It is** a pity that he will not share.
9. **I have** not seen the queen.
10. I **could not** eat all that!

Cross out the incorrect word to complete the sentences.

1. That isn't / is'nt my kitten.
2. We won't / wont' go out after all.
3. She doesn't / does'nt want to come to my party.
4. The birds weren't / were'nt eating the food I left out for them.
5. Whats / What's the matter?

Name: _____ Date: _____

1.5b (continued)

Apostrophes - contractions

Underline the correct **contraction** in these sentences.

1. **Id / I'd** like to cycle to school today.
2. **It's / Its** a shame that she hurt herself.
3. **He's / Hes** wearing a funny old hat!
4. If you don't wear any socks **you're / your** likely to get cold feet.

Now can you write your own short sentences using these **contractions**?

| I'm | Doesn't | He'll |
| That's | Who's | |

1. _____
2. _____
3. _____
4. _____
5. _____

Name: _____ Date: _____

2.1
Coordinating conjunction: **and**

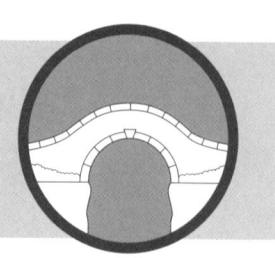

Use **and** to join the two parts of the sentence together.

1. Harry is wearing a hat _____ coat.

2. For breakfast, I had a banana _____ toast.

3. The toy robot can move _____ pick things up.

4. She ran faster than Sam _____ Nick.

5. Tess _____ Vicky are good friends.

6. I went to my friend's house _____ we played a lot of games.

7. The little boy let go of the balloon _____ it flew away.

8. The yeti lives over the hills _____ far away.

9. She likes eating peas _____ beans.

10. Walter likes playing _____ splashing in the water.

2.1 *(continued)*
Coordinating conjunction: **and**

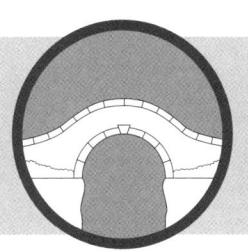

Using the conjunction **and**, join the two short sentences to make one long sentence. Check the **full stops** and **capital letters** are correct!

1. I went to the beach. I made a big sandcastle.

2. We ran into the sea. The waves were huge.

3. We went fishing in the rockpools. We found a crab.

4. The tide came in. It washed away my sand castle.

5. It got colder. Dad said it was time to go home.

Name: _____   Date: _____

2.1 (continued)

Coordinating conjunction: **and**

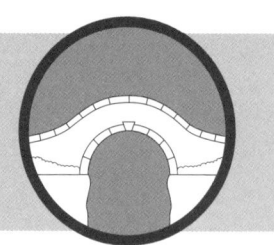

Can you write five sentences of your own using **and** to join groups of words together? Use the ideas below to help you.

Write a sentence about...

1. what you had for breakfast today.
2. the games you like playing.
3. the people you like.
4. your journey to school in the morning.
5. what you like to do at the weekend.

1. _____

2. _____

3. _____

4. _____

5. _____

Name: _____ Date: _____

2.2
Coordinating and subordinating conjunctions

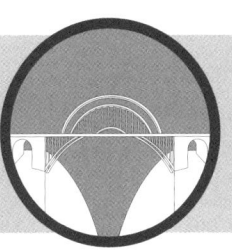

Use **but** to join these sentences. Write the new sentence underneath the old ones.

1. I would like to go in the water. I can't swim.

2. He would like to play football. He forgot his ball.

3. Tom tried to put up his umbrella. It was too windy.

Use **so** to join these sentences. Write the new sentence underneath the old ones.

1. This plate is dirty. I will get a new one.

2. It was a sunny day. They went for a walk.

3. The room was dark. Mum switched on the light.

Name: _____ Date: _____

2.2 (continued)

Coordinating and subordinating conjunctions

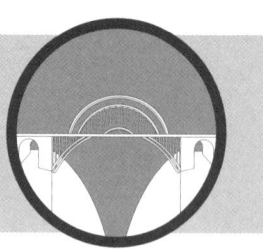

Choose the correct **conjunction** to join the two parts of each sentence together. Make sure you use each one *at least once*.

| so | but | or | and |

1. Sammy _____ Tess are coming with us.

2. Her cat prefers milk _____ water, but not both.

3. She was very hot _____ she jumped into the water.

4. Vicky would like to ride a horse _____ she doesn't know how to.

5. The light shines from the lighthouse _____ ships can find their way home.

6. Would you prefer a melon _____ would you prefer a marshmallow?

7. No-one knows how old that man is _____ we do know he is very wise.

8. The puppy likes jumping in the puddles _____ paddling in the pool.

Name: _____ Date: _____

2.2 (continued)

Coordinating and subordinating conjunctions

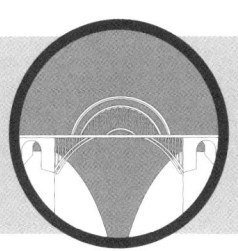

Choose the correct **conjunction** to join the two parts of each sentence together. Make sure you use each conjunction *at least once*.

| when | if | that | because |

1. He was walking along the path _____ he heard a strange sound.

2. Dad told me to pack my bags _____ we were going on holiday the next day.

3. Sammy can go to the pool _____ someone will take him.

4. She likes the hamster _____ is in the cage over there.

5. Vicky ran away _____ Walter was splashing too much.

6. We can go sledging down the hill _____ it snows.

7. You can have an ice cream _____ you work hard.

8. The cat _____ is very silly has climbed up the tree again.

Name: _____ Date: _____

2.3a
Nouns

Put a circle around the **nouns**.

cat　　tree　　pig　　went　　sit

cake　　jump　　pink　　warm　　baby

Draw a line to match the **noun** with its picture.

girl

puppy

ball

apple

drum

ink

Name: _____ Date: _____

2.3a *(continued)*
Nouns

Put a circle around the **noun** in each sentence. Be careful – sometimes there might be two!

1. He is called Dan.

2. That bird is very tiny.

3. I ate a banana.

4. The dog jumped up.

5. She has a new pencil.

6. Tess sat on a chair.

7. The boy played on the swing.

8. Mina lives in London.

9. The tree outside is good for climbing.

10. I went to the park with Mum.

2.3b
Simple noun phrases

Match the **simple noun phrase** to its picture.

a cute puppy

an interesting newspaper

a little boy

a big horse

....

Write a **noun phrase** for each of these pictures.

_____

_____

2.3c
Expanded noun phrases

Match the **expanded noun phrases** with the pictures.

the young girl that made the cake

the sleepy snake snoozed in the sun

the little bird that sat on the clock

the clever cat baked a cake

Can you spot the **noun phrase** in each of these sentences?
Put a circle around each one you find.

1. The stripy umbrella has blown away.

2. The boat with yellow sails belongs to Tess.

3. The man with the beard sells ice creams.

4. The girl wearing sunglasses is good at football.

5. The café in the park has the best cakes.

Name: _____ Date: _____

2.4
Statements, questions, exclamations, commands

Put a circle around the mark that shows whether the sentence is an **exclamation** or a **question**.

1. Who is that girl?
2. What time is it?
3. How awful!
4. Where are you?
5. She is so clever!
6. You are splashing me!
7. Can we go to see a film?
8. Is that your brother?
9. What a lovely day it is!
10. How exciting!

Put a line underneath the **statement**.

1. What time do we have to leave?
2. Please pass me that fork.
3. Leave me alone!
4. Everyone likes living in Letterland.

Put a line underneath the **command**.

1. Help me!
2. What are you doing?
3. Please put the flag up.
4. There is a bird in that tree.

30

Name: _____ Date: _____

2.4 (continued)
Statements, questions, exclamations, commands

What type of sentence are these Letterland characters saying?

- Never play with matches. — Firefighter Fred
- What fun it is to splash! — Walter Walrus
- Can I have a cup of tea? — Clever Cat
- My violets make me very happy. — Vicky Violet

1. Who is asking a **question**? _____

2. Who is giving a **command**? _____

3. Who is shouting an **exclamation**? _____

4. Who is making a **statement**? _____

31

Grammar Copymasters © Letterland International Ltd.

Name: _____   Date: _____

2.4 (continued)

Statements, questions, exclamations, commands

Write two **questions** to ask Harry Hat Man.

1. _____

2. _____

Write an **exclamation** for Nick's speech bubble.

What **command** is the mum giving to her children?

Write two **statements** about you:

1. _____

2. _____

Name: _____ Date: _____

3.1
Plural noun suffixes (-s or -es)

Add the suffix **-s** or **-es** to make these nouns plural.

1. **robot**
2. **girl**
3. **boy**
4. **cat**
5. **monster**

6. **fox**
7. **apple**
8. **cup**
9. **hose**
10. **bus**

Write the **plural** form of the underlined noun in these sentences.

1. Rosie baked a <u>cake</u>. _____

2. Ben likes riding his <u>bike</u>. _____

3. I played my <u>flute</u>. _____

4. Nick is banging a <u>nail</u>. _____

5. Vicky got on the <u>bus</u>. _____

6. They jumped out from behind the <u>bush</u>. _____

7. Look at the bright <u>torch</u>! _____

8. Who split the <u>glass</u> of water? _____

Name: _____ Date: _____

3.1 (continued)

Plural noun suffixes (-s or -es)

Make the sentence correct by adding the **plural** form of the noun in brackets.

1. Ben was hiding in the _____. (**box**)

2. Harry was wearing two _____. (**hat**)

3. Three _____ came along at once! (**bus**)

4. He has read so many _____. (**book**)

5. They are lots of _____ at the park. (**bench**)

6. The fairy gave me three _____. (**wish**)

7. They needed two _____ to take everyone on the school trip. (**coach**)

8. How many _____ are there in your name? (**letter**)

....

Can you write your own sentence using these nouns as **plurals**?

| balloon | dog | game | torch |

Name: _____   Date: _____

3.2a
Verbs

Put a circle around the **verbs**.

jump   run   table   sleep   wall

book   say   song   sing

Draw a line to match the **verbs** with the pictures.

sleep

feed

drive

kick

brush

sing

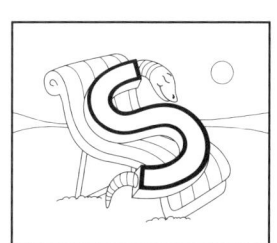

Name: _____ Date: _____

3.2a (continued)
Verbs

Underline the **verbs** in these sentences.

1. We walk to school when it is sunny.
2. Jim can jump very high.
3. The snake slithers over the hot sand.
4. Ben blows out the candles on his birthday cake.
5. Tess sends texts every day.
6. Ella can sing well.
7. I watch TV in the morning.
8. Walter splashes in the waves.
9. I would like to fly in a plane.
10. Jelly is my favourite thing to eat.

Write your own sentences using some of these **verbs**.

| skip | play | sit | think | look | cry |

_____

_____

_____

3.2b
Suffixes added to verbs

Underline the **suffix** at the end of each **verb**.
The suffix could be -**ed**, -**ing** or –**er**.

1. read**ing**
2. work**ed**
3. sleep**ing**
4. sing**er**
5. clean**ed**
6. lov**ed**
7. runn**er**
8. burn**ing**
9. read**er**
10. smell**ing**

Choose the correct **suffix** for the end of each verb: -**er**, -**ing** or -**ed**.

1. We walk____ to school yesterday.
2. When are you go____ to your granny's house?
3. Jim jump____ all the way down the road.
4. The walrus splash____ me.
5. I was watch____ my favourite programme on TV.
6. Ella is such a good sing____.
7. The plane is fly____ very high.
8. We need another play____ for our game.

Name: _____ Date: _____

3.2b *(continued)*
Suffixes added to verbs

Write the verb with the correct **suffix** in the gap.

1. The frog _____ off the log into the pond. (**jump**)

2. Kazuo's bike _____ along the track. (**bump**)

3. That morning Nick was _____ football in the garden. (**play**)

4. Asha was the only goal _____ in the match. (**score**)

5. Martin was _____ at something else. (**look**)

6. Yesterday I _____ my bedroom. (**clean**)

7. We need another _____ for our school trip. (**help**)

8. He _____ the ball so hard that it went through the window! (**kick**)

Write your own sentence using each **suffix** at the end of a **verb**.

-ing: _____

-er: _____

-ed: _____

3.3
Prefix un-

Add the **prefix un-** to these root words to give them the opposite meaning.

1. kind _____
2. fair _____
3. do _____
4. happy _____

5. tie _____
6. clean _____
7. pack _____
8. plug _____

Underline the **root word**.

unload   unable   unreal   unroll   unlucky

In these sentences, put a circle around the **prefix un-** and underline the root word.

1. Can you untie my laces, please?
2. It was unfair that she got three sweets and I only got two.
3. Mum said, "Don't be unkind to your sister."
4. If we unload the car we can put up the tent.
5. Now we have to unpack the shopping.
6. Unroll your sleeping bag and put it in the tent.

Name: _____   Date: _____

3.4 (Review)
Nouns and verbs

Can you remember the difference between **nouns** and **verbs**?

Put a circle around the **nouns** and underline the **verbs**.

bed   nest   bang   tail   cup   swim
vet   horse   see   sob   class paper

In these sentences, put a circle around the **nouns** and underline the **verbs**. Sometimes there might be more than one!

1. The bird chirped a sweet song.
2. Dan's alarm clock did not ring.
3. His cat makes me sneeze.
4. My dog always drinks water.
5. Ben throws a snowball.
6. Harry bumped into the table.
7. I want to take my cat to school.
8. The sun is very warm today.
9. They ran into the maze.
10. I pushed my sister down the snowy hill on a sledge.

Name: _____ Date: _____

3.4
Suffixes to form nouns: -er, -ness

Add the suffix -**er** or -**ness** to make these sentences correct.

1. The night sky was under a cover of black____.

2. Dad needs to find a buy____ for his old car.

3. The bright____ of the sunshine lit up my bedroom.

4. There is a nasty sick____ going around.

5. Ben is such a good sing____.

6. I cried with sad____ when I lost my teddy.

7. Our teach____ is the best in the school!

8. That climb____ can get all the way to the top of the mountain.

9. The old lady showed me lots of kind____ by helping me find my teddy.

10. The damp____ of the cave made him shiver.

Name: _____ Date: _____

3.4 *(continued)*

Suffixes to form nouns: **-ness**, -er

Add the suffix **-er** to these verbs to make a noun. Remember you only need to use the **r** of the suffix as the **e** is already there!

Verb	Noun
write	
bake	
dive	
make	
drive	
joke	
rule	

Add the suffix **-er** to these verbs to make a noun. Remember to double the consonant before adding the suffix.

Verb	Noun
run	
rub	
swim	
rob	

Name: _____ Date: _____

3.4 (continued)

Suffixes to form nouns: -ness, -er

Add the suffix -**er** to these verbs to make the sentences correct.
Don't forget to check your spellings.

1. The swim____ dived into the water.

2. Clever Cat is a great bake____.

3. Tess is the fastest run____ I have ever seen.

4. Fred is the drive____ of the fire engine.

5. Red robot is a cunning rob____!

6. When I grow up, I would like to be a write____.

43

Grammar Copymasters © Letterland International Ltd.

3.5
Compound nouns (one word)

Put a circle around the **nouns**.

foot   yellow   book   sing

try   case   room

ball   run   soft   bed

brush   make   tooth

Look at the nouns you have circled. Which four **compound nouns** can you make with them?

1. _____

2. _____

3. _____

4. _____

Name: _____ Date: _____

3.5 (continued)
Compound nouns (one word)

Join the words to make **compound nouns** that are *one word*.

white	time
hair	room
tooth	boy
cow	time
skate	paste
sea	board
bath	shell
watch	man
bed	dog
snow	cut

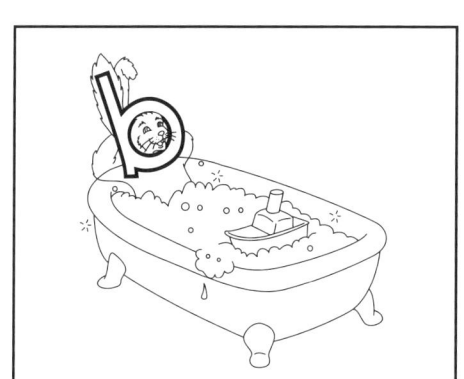

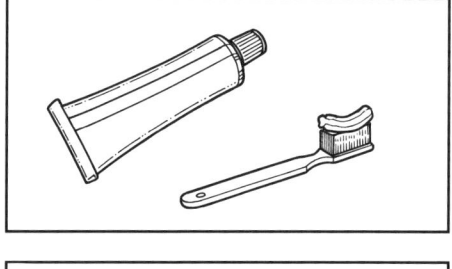

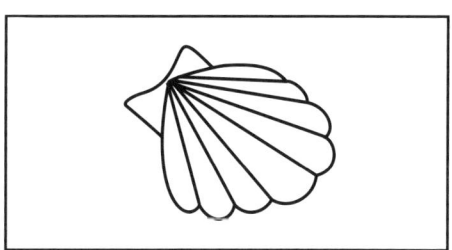

Write the **compound nouns** you have made here.

1. _____   6. _____

2. _____   7. _____

3. _____   8. _____

4. _____   9. _____

5. _____   10. _____

3.5 (continued)

Compound nouns (two words)

Join the words to make **compound nouns** that are *two words*.

Write your new **compound nouns** here.

bus	juice	1. _____
swimming	case	2. _____
apple	stop	3. _____
pencil	machine	4. _____
washing	car	5. _____
rowing	boat	6. _____
racing	pool	7. _____

Underline the eight **compound nouns** in this piece of writing. Some are one word, some have a space between them.

It was a bad day. First, my alarm clock did not wake me up. My bedroom door was closed. When I turned the doorknob it came off in my hand! When mum opened the door, I ran into the bathroom. I tried to brush my teeth, but the toothpaste had run out. I grabbed my pencil case and ran to the bus stop. Oh no! The school bus had just left.

Name: _____ Date: _____

3.6
Suffixes to form adjectives: -ful, -less

Change these words to **adjectives** by adding the suffix -**ful**.

1. help _____
2. care _____
3. use _____
4. cup _____
5. thank _____
6. hand _____
7. beauty _____
8. plate _____

Choose four of the **adjectives** you have made and write a sentence using each one.

1. _____
2. _____
3. _____
4. _____

Change these words to **adjectives** by adding the suffix -**less**.

1. help _____
2. hope _____
3. care _____
4. tooth _____
5. use _____
6. life _____
7. thank _____
8. harm _____

Choose four of the **adjectives** you have made and write a sentence using each one.

1. _____
2. _____
3. _____
4. _____

Name: _____ Date: _____

3.6 (continued)

Suffixes to form adjectives: -**ful**, -**less**

Complete the words in these sentences by using the suffix -**ful** or -**less**.

1. The cat was help____, stuck up in the tree.

2. The tooth____ dragon cannot bite us.

3. Take a hand____ of popcorn.

4. With that big smile on her face, Vicky looks very cheer____ today.

5. Yuck. This weak tea is taste____.

6. Don't worry, those spiders are harm____.

7. He can't talk because he has a mouth____ of chocolate cake.

8. Be care____ when you sit in the sun.

Name: _____ Date: _____

3.7
Suffixes to form adjectives: -er, -est

Add the suffix **-er** or **-est** to describe the pictures. The first one has been done to help you.

The butterfly is smaller than the frog, but the bee is the smallest.

....

The snake is long____ than the worm, but the hose is the long____.

....

The girl is young____ than her mum, but her baby brother is the young____.

....

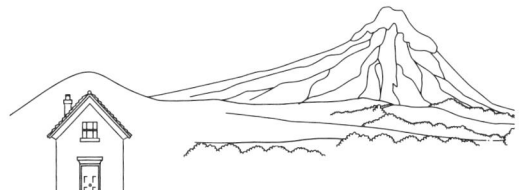

The hill is high____ than the house, but the mountain is high____.

....

Now you try! Draw a picture in the box.

_____

_____

3.7 (continued)

Suffixes to form adjectives: -er, -est

Fill in the gaps in these sentences with the suffix -**er** or -**est**.

1. My friend Jack is not the tall____ person I know, but he is the kind____.

2. I think that Jack is kind____ than Ali.

3. That cat is the clever____ animal I have ever seen!

4. Tess is in a hurry so she walks the quick____ way into town.

5. Could you put the hook low____ so that the children can reach it?

6. Is this book short____ than that one?

7. Anna is the fast____ runner in the class.

8. She is a fast____ runner than I am.

Name: _____ Date: _____

3.7 (continued)
Suffixes to form adjectives: -er, -est

Sometimes spellings change when you are using the suffixes -**er** and -**est**.
Before adding the suffix:
- some words need an extra consonant at the end e.g. big/big**g**er/big**g**est
- if the word ends in **e**, drop it off
- if a word ends in **y**, change the **y** to **i** e.g. funn**y**/funn**i**er/funn**i**est

Add the suffix -**er** to these words. Be careful to check the spelling.

1. happy _____
2. huge _____
3. long _____
4. smelly _____
5. high _____
6. pretty _____
7. hot _____
8. short _____
9. flat _____
10. mad _____

Add the suffix -**est** to these words. Be careful to check the spelling.

1. silly _____
2. clever _____
3. fit _____
4. flat _____
5. kind _____
6. big _____
7. shiny _____
8. nice _____
9. fat _____
10. huge _____

Name: _____ Date: _____

3.7 (continued)
Suffixes to form adjectives: -er, -est

Fill in the gap in the sentences using the correct suffix for the root word.

1. That clown is the _____. (**silly**)

2. That apple is _____ than the other one. (**shiny**)

3. Harry's house is _____ than Ben's house. (**big**)

4. It is the _____ day we have had this year! (**hot**)

5. We are getting _____ up the hill. (**high**)

6. The more my cat eats, the _____ she gets. (**fat**)

7. That is the _____ giant I have ever seen! (**big**)

8. I think that dress is _____ than the shirt. (**nice**)

9. Let's camp over there where the ground is _____ than it is here. (**flat**)

10. The mouse is _____ than the rat. (**small**)

3.8
Suffixes to form adverbs: -ly

Adverbs *describe* **verbs** – they tell us how the verb is being done.

Put a circle around the **verbs**. Underline the **adverbs**.

quietly   run   make   loudly   quack

gently   knock   quickly   fall

Which suffix do you notice at the end of each of the adverbs?

_____

Match the **adverb** to describe each **verb**.

run	loudly
make	quickly
sleep	neatly
write	carefully
eat	peacefully
talk	greedily

3.8 (continued)

Suffixes to form adverbs: -ly

Change these **adjectives** to **adverbs** by adding the suffix –**ly**.

1. kind _____
2. quiet _____
3. quick _____
4. slow _____
5. loud _____
6. soft _____
7. careful _____

Choose two of the **adverbs** you have made and write a sentence for each one. *Example: He ran down the stairs quickly.*

1. _____

2. _____

Put a circle around all the **adverbs** ending with -**ly** in this piece of writing. There are seven adverbs in total.

I have a puppy called Daisy. She barks loudly when the postman comes. If I say softly, "Daisy, shhh." She quickly stops and wags her tail. On Sunday we went for a walk. She ran off happily along the track and jumped lightly over all the puddles. Then she rolled over playfully for me to tickle her tummy.

Name: _____ Date: _____

3.8 (continued)
Suffixes to form adverbs: -ly

Sometimes spellings change when you use the suffix -ly to make an adverb
Before adding the suffix:
- if a word ends in **y**, change the **y** to **i**
- if a word ends in **le**, drop off the **e**
- if a word ends in **ic**, add -**ally**

Let's practise! Add the suffix -**ly** to make these words **adverbs**.
Be careful to check the spelling.

1. happy _____

2. short _____

3. simple _____

4. terrible _____

5. high _____

6. pretty _____

7. hot _____

8. gentle _____

9. basic _____

Name: _____ Date: _____

3.8 (continued)
Suffixes to form adverbs: -ly

Fill in the gap in the sentences using the suffix -ly. Check the spelling!

1. _____, I forgot my glasses. (**stupid**)

2. Ugh, that lemon was _____ bitter. (**horrible**)

3. He _____ brought a rabbit out from up his sleeve. (**magical**)

4. I would _____ eat ice cream for breakfast! (**happy**)

5. The hill behind his house slopes up _____. (**steep**)

6. The dog growled _____ when it saw next door's cat. (**angry**)

7. "Can we go to the cinema?" I asked _____. (**hopeful**)

8. We were _____ late for the show. (**terrible**)

9. The baby ate his mashed banana very _____. (**messy**)

10. Mum _____ wiped his mouth. (**gentle**)

Name: _____ Date: _____

4.1
Present and past tenses

Match the verb in the **present** tense to the correct picture. Write it underneath.

laughs   runs   cooks   pats   points   yawns

_____   _____   _____

_____   _____   _____

Change the **present** tense verbs to the **past** tense.

1. laughs _____
2. points _____
3. yawns _____
4. cooks _____
5. likes _____

6. talks _____
7. washes _____
8. types _____
9. smiles _____
10. bakes _____

57

Name: _____ Date: _____

4.1 (continued)
Present and past tenses

Match the **present** and **past** tense verbs.

kicks	pulled
shivers	opened
pulls	filled
opens	jumped
jumps	juggled
enjoys	kicked
fills	enjoyed
juggles	shivered

Write these verbs in the **present** tense and the **past** tense. Be careful of the spelling changes!

Verb	Present Tense	Past Tense
try	she _____	she _____
cry	the baby _____	the baby _____
dry	he _____	he _____
get	Tess _____	Tess _____
see	Nick _____	Nick _____
run	Ben _____	Ben _____
say	the King _____	the King _____
write	the Queen _____	the Queen _____
eat	Fred _____	Fred _____
throw	Lucy _____	Lucy _____
go	Harry _____	Harry _____
hop	Jim _____	Jim _____

Name: _____ Date: _____

4.1 (continued)

Present and past tenses

The correct verbs are missing in this piece of writing.
Add the verbs in the **present** tense.

| play | give | be | run | like |

Ben _____ with the baby bunny.

He _____ her a hug. The bunny _____ Ben.

Over there a puppy _____ with a pony.

They _____ happy.

Now fill in the verbs again, but this time put them in the **past** tense.

| play | give | be | run | like |

Ben _____ with the baby bunny.

He _____ her a hug. The bunny _____ Ben.

Over there a puppy _____ with a pony.

They _____ happy.

Name: _____ Date: _____

4.1 *(continued)*
Present and past tenses

Write three things that you are doing at the moment. Make sure you write them in the **present** tense.

1. At the moment, I _____

_____

2. At the moment, I _____

_____

3. At the moment, I _____

_____

• •

Write three things that you did yesterday. Make sure you write them in the **past** tense.

1. Yesterday, I _____

_____

2. Yesterday, I _____

_____

3. Yesterday, I _____

_____

Grammar Copymasters © Letterland International Ltd.

4.2
Present progressive and past tenses

Fill in the gaps with the **present progressive** form of each verb.

1. Ben ___ _____ his ball. (**bounce**)

2. Jim ___ _____ all over the place. (**jump**)

3. Wait a minute, she ___ _____ her shoelaces. (**tie**)

4. Walter ___ _____ a little tune. (**hum**)

5. All the birds ___ _____ on the wire. (**sit**)

6. I have my umbrella up because it ___ _____. (**rain**)

7. The wind ___ _____ so hard the trees ___ _____ ! (**blow/bend**)

8. Vicky and Max ___ _____ on the ice. (**skate**)

4.2 (continued)

Present progressive and past tenses

Write a sentence to describe what is happening in each picture. Remember to use the **present progressive** form.

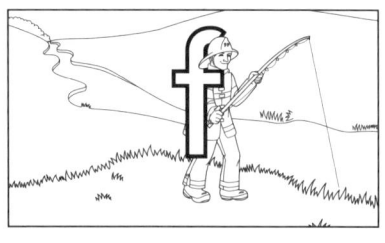   He is fishing in the river.

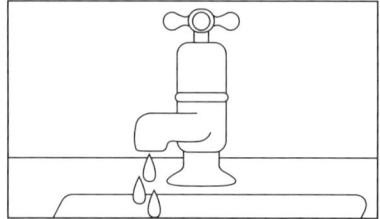

4.2 (continued)
Present progressive and past tenses

Fill in the gaps with the **past progressive** form of each verb, e.g. *The boys <u>were</u> talking.*

1. Ben ___ _____ his ball when I called him. (**bounce**)

2. Yesterday, Jim ___ _____ all over the place. (**jump**)

3. We were late because she ___ _____ her shoelaces. (**tie**)

4. Walter ___ _____ himself in a waterfall. (**wash**)

5. All the birds ___ _____ on the wire. (**sit**)

6. Yesterday, they ___ _____ the same shoes. (**wear**)

7. It ___ _____ when I left the house this morning. (**rain**)

8. When I saw Vicky, she ___ _____ along the path. (**run**)

9. The two of us ___ _____ out, when the phone rang. (**go**)

10. On Friday, the wind ___ _____ so hard that it was difficult to stand up! (**blow**)

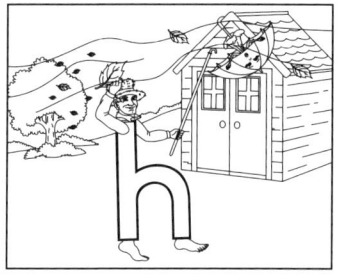

4.2 (continued)

Present progressive and past tenses

Fill in the gaps in this story with **present** and **past progressive** verbs. The words in the box are in order to help you. Be careful to get the right tense!

| tie   hang   decorate   use   going   do   make   try   come |

On Saturday, it was Ben's birthday. His brothers decided to give him a surprise party. They invited Vicky and Nick to help them get ready. When Vicky opened the door, she saw Berny, who ____ _____ up blue balloons. Blake ____ _____ them up. The third brother, Bobby, ____ _____ the birthday cake. He ____ _____ icing to write the words 'Happy Birthday Ben'.

  "We ____ _____ to help," said Vicky, "But it looks like you ____ _____ just fine!"
"Thanks," said Bobby, "But I ____ _____ a bit of a mess! Can you write more neatly with icing?" He handed over to Vicky to have a go.
  "Look at that!" laughed Nick. "I ____ _____ my best," Vicky said crossly. At last, everyone had finished their jobs. Vicky looked out of the window and saw that Ben ____ _____ down the road. He opened the door. "Surprise!" everyone shouted.